THE MAN
— of —
SORROWS
and
— ONE —
PILGRIM'S JOURNEY

foreword & edited by
JOANNE CASH

A NEVER-BEFORE PUBLISHED INSIDER'S
LOOK AT JOHNNY CASH'S FINAL DAYS
BASED ON THE PERSONAL
LOG OF JIMMY TITTLE

by
BRIAN OXLEY

OXVISION
BOOKS

ISBN 978 1 938068 30 0

Library of Congress Control Number: 2018942151

© 2018 Oxvision Books
All Rights Reserved. No part of this book or site may be reproduced or redistributed in any form or by any electronic or mechanical means, including information storage and retrieval systems, without permission in writing from Oxvision Media, LLC, except by a reviewer who may quote brief passages in a review.

Published by Oxvision Books
Oxvision Media, LLC, 4001 Tamiami Trail North, Suite 250, Naples, FL 34103

Find us at: **oxvisionmedia.com**

TABLE OF CONTENTS

FOREWORD	By Joanne Cash		xi
INTRODUCTION	The Man in Black and *The Hound of Heaven*		xv
CHAPTER 1	Humble Beginnings		1
CHAPTER 2	Temptation in the Wilderness		5
CHAPTER 3	Water into Wine		9
CHAPTER 4	A Record Catch		13
CHAPTER 5	The Healing Touch		17
CHAPTER 6	Leader of Leaders		21
CHAPTER 7	Calm in the Storm		27
CHAPTER 8	Mercy		31
CHAPTER 9	Blind But Now I See		35
CHAPTER 10	Man of Sorrows, Man in Black		41
CHAPTER 11	Let the Children Come		45
CHAPTER 12	Confronting the Moneychangers		49
CHAPTER 13	Gifts from the Heart		55
CHAPTER 14	In the Garden		61
CHAPTER 15	Two Opposite Kinds of Shame		67
CHAPTER 16	Mary Magdalene		73
CHAPTER 17	A Shepherd's Heart		79
CHAPTER 18	Road to Damascus		85
CHAPTER 19	An Old Man's Final Task		91
CHAPTER 20	The Man Comes Around		97
CONCLUSION	An Insider's Look...		101

*He was despised and rejected of men,
a man of sorrows, and acquainted with grief.*

Isaiah 53:3

FOREWORD

FOREWORD BY JOANNE CASH

THIS BOOK IS INTENDED TO show some of the connections between the Man of Sorrows (Jesus) and one pilgrim's journey to and with the Man of Sorrows. That pilgrim in this particular book just happens to be my brother, Johnny Cash. His journey and mine are so, so similar that I believe that I can tell the story almost better than anyone else.

In this book we retell some of the experiences from the life of Jesus in a way that we hope will help readers to see Him as He really was—perhaps for the first time. Then we share some of the experiences from Johnny's life. It is in no way trying to compare their lives as equal, but rather to show that Jesus walked this earth in such a way that anyone can follow His tracks and become the person that God wants them to be. And that includes any and all readers of this book.

Johnny was such a giver. I have seen his compassion in so many ways over the years. The story about the family with the load of wood in chapter 5 is such a great example of his love to help the poor and needy. He never made a difference in how he valued people because of how much money they had. He treated the beggar on the street the same as the Queen of England. He showed mercy and forgiveness to all, even to those who took from him. Yes, people stole from him and used him. He just forgave them and loved them.

I John 1:9 says, "If you will confess your sins, God is faithful and just to forgive us our sins, and to cleanse us from all unrighteousness." Johnny told my husband Harry and me one day, "I know people use me and that's ok. I forgive them. But it's when I don't know and I find out—that's when it really hurts."

Jesus said, "Suffer the little children to come unto me and forbid them not, for of such is the kingdom of heaven." God loves all of us. He doesn't just do love. He is love. He is the essence of love itself.

Johnny was a father. He loved his children and his family, but because of his fame, it was often hard to spend quality time with just him and his children. That's why the farm became such a great place to just be a Daddy and hang out with them. God sees the heart of us all. He sees our need, our want, and our motive. He knows and understands the reasons why we do the things we do.

Johnny was human. He made mistakes and was the first to admit it, but his heart was a heart of caring. He shared his love for the farm with his family members. It became his spiritual hideaway. I am Joanne, the youngest Cash sister. Often, Harry and I would go and spend three or four days at the farm just to rest and get away from the phone. We are pastors of a growing church, and we sometimes need to get away, and pray and rest as well.

One Thanksgiving, we took 10 of the youth from our church to the farm and stayed for three days. We drove all over those 100 acres in Johnny's red jeep and explored the caves in the back of the property. We cooked turkey with all the trimmings, we sang and went barefoot, and we just hung out and got to just be ourselves.

Our parents have long since passed away—Daddy on December 23, 1985, and Mama on March 11, 1991. I remember the dream/vision in chapter 18 of this book that Johnny had on Christmas night in 1985, two days after Daddy's death. I was in awe, realizing it was not just a dream, but a message from heaven. When Johnny told Mama, she cried and so did I.

Jesus Christ is the King of Kings and Lord of Lords. There's none to compare to Him. My brother, as well as you and I, are humans created by God in His image. Johnny patterned his life to walk the way that Jesus would have him walk. As his sister, I believe that in every situation he faced, he stopped and asked himself, "Okay, Cash, what would Jesus do?" Then he tried his best to do just that.

I am so grateful to be Johnny's sister. I learned so much from him. We walked down some of the same dark and drug-filled roads, but like the Apostle Paul, we both experienced that life-changing light of mercy and forgiveness.

John, I'll see you in heaven and we'll walk barefoot together by the crystal river!

INTRODUCTION

The Man in Black and *The Hound of Heaven*

*I fled Him, down the nights and down the days;
I fled Him, down the arches of the years.*

From "The Hound of Heaven"
Written by Francis Thompson (1859–1907)

THESE LINES WERE NEVER SUNG by Johnny Cash, but they could well have been, for the great Hound of Heaven that pursued the popular Victorian poet Francis Thompson, pursued Cash just as relentlessly.

The story of that pursuit—of where and how the Man in Black fled, and how he became utterly lost, and then was found—is the story behind all of the stories Johnny sang about.

Cash opens chapter 6 of his autobiography by telling us how there came a time in his life when he was taking amphetamines and barbiturates by the handful and as a result frequently had to cancel shows and recording dates.

"And when I did show up, I couldn't sing because my throat was too dried out from the pills," he reports.

"There was nothing left of me," Cash goes on to confess as he walked down the same path of addiction and despair that Francis Thompson had found himself on a century before. "At that moment I was as far from God as I have ever been."

But just when Johnny Cash's separation from God seemed finally complete, it turned out that it wasn't.

"I'd thought I'd left Him," Cash writes, "but He hadn't left me."

In the years that followed, Johnny Cash would often perform Hank Williams' great song of faith "I Saw the Light." And when he did, John added a new verse he had written that described his own story. In it he tells of a time when he was in darkness and had no idea where the way out could be. But finally came a sunrise that rolled back the night and then, as Cash reports, "Praise the Lord, I saw the light."

The book you hold in your hands is a type rarely seen anymore. But if you were to travel back to Europe during the 16th century, you would find that Emblem books—books that tell a story with words and pictures in equal roles—were all the rage. The Emblem combination of picture and text was intended to live on not just in the mind, but also in the heart and soul.

The book in your hands could be said to be a modern day Emblem book. It contains images that reflect the life of Jesus— the real Jesus—who was true God and true Man. It also contains words that combine with the pictures to bring to life the real story of the Man of Sorrows and the Man in Black that He came to seek and to save.

CHAPTER 1

Humble Beginnings

"Joseph, I'm tired. Take him."

MARY'S WORDS BROKE INTO HIS thoughts. Me? Hold Him? The brawny village carpenter tried hard to smile and look confident and to hide how weary and worn down he really was.

Somehow he had gotten his expecting wife safely to Bethlehem, but again and again was told, "No room!" Finally, he had been offered a place, but only a pen for animals, not proper housing for his exhausted bride and the divine treasure she carried. Again and again, he fought back the dark feelings of failure.

Joseph gently cradled the newborn babe in his arms. And then came the second miracle on that miraculous night. As Joseph looked down at the tiny face, slowly, all the fears of the past months began to drain out of him and something in his heart leapt. He felt strength flow through his veins as the first real smile in a long time spread over his face.

Unto us a child is born, he thought of the words from the sacred scriptures as he held the baby to his chest. *Unto us a son is given.* And he whispered the words again with joy. *A son is given!*

Ray Cash married Carrie Rivers on August 18, 1920. She was 16, and he was 23. Ray had been working a series of odd jobs, and they had met when he had boarded with her family while he was cutting lumber for a bridge that was to span a nearby river.

Twelve years later, on a cold February night, Carrie gave birth to an 11-pound boy they called "J.R." It was the height of the Great Depression, and there was little food or comfort to spare. When the cold wind blew from the north, Carrie draped blankets on the splintered inside walls of their tiny shotgun house to try to keep it out.

Every day more and more poor farmers like Ray were put out of work as cotton prices fell lower and lower. Every day more and more of their neighbors packed what little they had and left Arkansas to seek better luck in California. Ray and Carrie did not move, but often he was forced to climb inside a slow-moving boxcar as it passed near their home and to ride the rails in search of work to support his growing family.

Few of us would intentionally choose such humble beginnings and all the hardships that come with them. But for the son of a carpenter and the son of a cotton farmer, humble beginnings were followed by a life of compassion for the poor and beaten-down, and a commitment to never forget the hungry or the hopeless.

CHAPTER 2

Temptation in the Wilderness

HE WAS HUNGRY, HUNGRY IN a way that should have a different word to describe it than the one we use when we skip breakfast or our supper is late. He was hungry and weak, and worst of all, He was alone—totally alone in the vast, desert wilderness. Such moments are always preferred by the tempter.

All at once, He was transported to the peak of a tall mountain. Around Him, Jesus could see all the kingdoms of the world sparkling like jewels in their splendor. "God's Son," said the voice. "All these I will give you—if only you will bow down and worship me."

Just a quick, little bow, and then, and then… No years of itinerate preaching and the exhaustion and derision that would come with it as He went from town to town. No rejection, no betrayal, and most of all no agonizing death upon the cross.

"Be gone!" Christ shouted with resolution and authority. "It is written, worship the Lord God and serve Him only!"

Immediately the voice was gone and Jesus was alone once more on the desert floor. Looking at the ground in front of Him, He smiled a wry smile—the stones were still there. The temptation was over, for now. And then suddenly angels were there bringing Him food and comfort.

In his autobiography, Johnny Cash tells how there came a time when he was taking amphetamines and barbiturates by the handful. After a trail of car wrecks, trips to jail, and visits to the hospital, he found himself scraping, as he puts it, the filthy bottom of the barrel of life. Finally hitting a point where he did not want to see another dawn, he drove to Tennessee's Nickajack Cave, tempted to end it all.

Johnny crawled into the vast, winding cavern for two or three hours until the batteries in his flashlight finally went out, and then laid down in the total darkness to die. And there when his separation from God seemed finally complete, it turned out that it wasn't.

Alone, but not alone in the inky blackness, Johnny gradually felt a sensation of complete peace fill his ravaged body and troubled mind. And as his thoughts were drawn to God, he became aware of one simple fact. His life, his death, his success, everything—it was all in the hands of One greater than him and always had been.

Responding to a mysterious urging, he began crawling in the

total darkness, not even knowing which direction he was headed. After some time he felt the gentle breath of wind on his back and followed it until finally, off in the distance, he saw the faint light of the cave's opening. Miraculously, Johnny Cash had found his way out of the darkness of Nickajack Cave, but it was inside the cave that the real miracle had happened and a wayward soul had been found. Much later in life, he had six ornamental angels permanently installed on the front of the farmhouse at Bon Aqua—a reminder of the constant watch our guardian angels keep over us day and night.

CHAPTER 3

Water into Wine

ALL WEDDINGS ARE BEAUTIFUL, MARY thought, but this one had been particularly lovely. She was close to both families and knew what this day had meant to them. Everything had turned out perfectly, she was about to say, when she noticed two anxious-looking servers next to the wine containers.

They've run out of wine! Mary suddenly realized with the kind of knot in her stomach only a poor mother could have. The parents would be so ashamed if they were not able to provide this feast for their guests. What to do? Mary turned to her son seated next to her.

"They've run out of wine," she whispered so only He would hear. Then she motioned to the servers to come over and told them, "Do whatever he tells you to do."

Mary knew her son. She was sure He would see the problem and was certain He would do something to help.

"Fill those containers to the brim with water," Jesus said, indicating six large stone jars standing near the entrance. "When you finish, draw some out and take it to the master of the feast." There was a quiet confidence in His voice, and the servers quickly obeyed. Jesus finished the story He had been telling and then slipped away. He wanted to be there to see the banquet master's reaction.

The steward of the feast took a small sip and then another. With each taste his eyes grew wider and the look on his face more astonished. It was the best wine he had ever tasted! In answer to the servers' questioning looks, the flabbergasted banquet master waved for them to begin filling the guests' empty cups.

With all the celebrating, Mary was the only one who noticed Jesus off to the side watching with amusement. How He loved helping people! Of all the things Mary kept in her heart from that day, her most cherished memory was the pure delight she had seen in her beloved son's eyes.

We are only three pages into the Bon Aqua section of Johnny Cash's autobiography when we are told about the special place near the farmhouse where Johnny planted grapes. He makes it clear that tending the vines at Bon Aqua was a big part of what made the place so important to him. He tells readers:

"I put them in three years ago, with cuttings I took from my vines at my home in Hendersonville, which in turn grew from cuttings I took from my parents' arbor in California in 1968 and carried back to Tennessee wrapped in wet newspaper inside a suitcase."

He concludes, "I love taking care of my vines, then having them take care of me."

Luther Fleaner, who looked after the arbor when Johnny was away, recalls, "He'd call me from California or anywhere he was at, and ask, 'How's my grapes?'"

In the video from his concert at San Quentin, Johnny Cash tells of a moment of divine inspiration that took place when he and June visited the town of Canaan and found the church built over the cistern where the water came from that Christ turned to wine 2,000 years before.

Johnny described how in the crypt below he saw the ancient container and heard the sound of the water and the echo it made. He explained, "If I ever had an inspiration, I had one then from seeing what I had just seen and heard." As Johnny and June left the church, he said softly, "He turned the water into wine of all things."

In the car on the way to Tiberius, Johnny wrote the song "He Turned the Water into Wine"—his tribute to Christ's first miracle.

CHAPTER 4

A Record Catch

ONE DAY JESUS TOOK A walk by the Sea of Galilee. Soon people started to recognize Him and a crowd began to grow. Jesus looked about and saw two boats tied at the water's edge while the fishermen who owned them washed their nets. He got into the boat that belonged to Simon and asked him to push out a little way from the shore, so He could talk to the people that way.

After He had finished teaching, Jesus turned to Simon and said, "Take us out where the water is deeper and let down your nets."

"Master," Simon answered, trying not to appear disrespectful, "we were out all last night and did not catch a single thing."

What did this carpenter from Nazareth know about catching fish, the experienced seaman wondered. Everyone knew going out in the heat of the day was pointless, and Simon had just finished putting up the clean nets. But looking into the Teacher's eyes, he saw something that made him add, "But if you say so, I will let down the nets again."

Minutes later, Simon's nets were in the water. As he began to pull them in, he could feel fish wiggling and pulling. Lots of fish. As they neared the surface and took on their full weight, the nets became so heavy he and his crew could not lift them any higher.

"James! John! Get out here!" Simon yelled to his companions. Soon both boats were so full of fish that their sides dipped dangerously close to the water's surface.

Only then did what had happened fully register with Simon as he recognized the presence of the Divine in the boat with him and his own unworthiness. Wiping his hands on his apron, he fell at Jesus' feet and pleaded, "Go away from me, Lord. I am too much of a sinner to be around you."

"Do not be afraid, Simon," the Lord said, "from now on you will catch men."

Simon, James, and John pulled their boats up on the shore, and leaving everything behind—their boats, nets, and all the fish—Jesus' first disciples followed Him.

In the opening chapter of *Man in Black*, Johnny describes a group of people that he refers to as "Johnny Cash Watchers." These are people who became frustrated with him because of the great change that had come about in his life, a change they neither understood nor liked.

"They want me to be like I was," John reports. "They want to hear me curse again. They want me to wear a black hat and wreck my car and fail to show up at concerts."

The truth John goes on to say, as hard and heavy as it may seem, is that, "If you're going to be a Christian you're going to change. You're going to lose some old friends."

"When Christ calls a man, he bids him come and die." Dietrich Bonhoeffer wrote this now famous line in his classic work *The Cost of Discipleship*. The vast majority of Christians will not be called to die the death of a martyr, but instead to die to their old selves, their old habits, and their old priorities.

In this encounter with Jesus, as the three future disciples have one of their best catches ever—a record catch the Gospels report—we see them leaving everything from their old life behind as they turn from their old purpose of catching fish to sell in the marketplace to saving men's souls.

"Follow me and I will make you fishers of men."

"When Christ calls a man, he bids him come and die."

On the final page of *Man in Black*, Johnny describes the new path he is on this way: "I really don't know what direction my life is going to take from here. I just know I'm on the track. Whatever He's got planned for me, I'm ready to listen. I'm ready to try to follow."

CHAPTER 5

The Healing Touch

LOOK DEEPLY, IF YOU CAN, at the man with leprosy. Look beyond his dirty rags and diseased skin and see the defeat in his eyes. See a man who is on the verge of simply giving up.

People kept their distance. Anyone who got too near risked becoming an outcast themselves. Totally despised, he was also totally without hope, for there was no known cure for leprosy except the grave.

But then one day, he heard amazing news. Jesus, the one some were calling the Messiah, was coming near that day! The leper made his way to the Master and in utter desperation cried out, "Lord, if you will, you can make me clean." The leper recognized that Jesus had the power to heal his affliction. But why would He?

Little did he know that the Lord of the Universe was

also Lord of the Outcast and that He specialized in bringing hope to the hopeless.

Now look at Jesus. He looks directly at the man, seeing him as someone of great value. See how Jesus gives the man His complete attention. As Jesus senses the years of heartache and despair, His face fills with compassion. Jesus could have kept His distance and simply ignored him. Or if He had wanted, He could have healed the man's ailment with a word. But instead, He draws close, closer than anyone has been in a long time—for there is something more to heal. And then Jesus does what no one has dared to do. He stretches out His hand and tenderly touches him.

And with this touch, the man who was once seen as untouchable is given back his dignity and is healed body and soul.

GRANDPA AND THE MAN SELLING FIREWOOD
by Thomas Gabriel

I'm not 100 percent sure on the date, but it was winter. It had started to snow pretty hard, and so school was being let out early before the roads got so bad the busses wouldn't be able to run.

Grandpa picked us up, and we went through the McDonald's drive through in Hendersonville. I had barely opened my food when Grandpa suddenly got into the left lane and made a U-turn. I looked up to see what was going on and saw a man and his family on the side of the road selling firewood. Their truck was still completely full. Whether people did not like his looks or just didn't need any firewood, no one had stopped to buy any.

The man looked dirty, cold, and tired. His truck was well over its load capacity, and looked like it should have been retired decades before. I sat in the car eating while Grandpa got out and spoke with the man.

I watched them talk and saw my Grandpa pointing in the direction of home. In a minute or so we were back on our way, but I noticed Grandpa was driving a little slower and was watching in the rear view. So, I turned to see at what he was looking at. The-terribly-overloaded-should-have-been-retired-decades-ago truck and the family who accompanied it were behind us, following us home.

We got to Grandpa's house, and I was still not very interested in the wood, the truck, or the family, so I went about my business in the house where it was warm. After a few hours passed, I went outside and noticed that the truck was still there, although it was now empty. I went back in and asked why the beat up old truck was still in the driveway.

Grandpa tossed the keys to me and said, "I bought it." Holding the keys I was even more curious and confused.

Grandpa said for me to take it over to the compound across from the main house—the fenced in land where he had his animals—and to put it by the first barn. I did, but only after I and a fellow young family member and a school friend put it through about an hour's abuse. That was the last time that truck ever ran.

I later found out that Grandpa had paid the man what he thought was a fair price for his wood plus enough to buy the man a better work truck and to pay for a ride to buy that new truck.

I always thought that must have been a great feeling for everyone involved, especially Grandpa.

CHAPTER 6

Leader of Leaders

AFTER FINISHING THE MOST FAMOUS sermon of His ministry, Jesus came down from the mountains outside Capernaum and entered the town. Immediately He was approached by a delegation of the local Jewish elders with an urgent request.

"Teacher, we come on behalf of a Roman Centurion who is a good friend to us and to the Jews. He has a servant who is very dear to him who is sick and near death. Our friend asks you to take pity and heal this one who is so beloved by him."

A high-ranking officer in the Roman army who is a friend to Jews? A man of wealth and prestige who is so worried about the health of one servant that he sends a special envoy to plead for help?

"He loves our nation and has built our synagogue,"

one of the elders added. An exceptional man, Jesus thought, and immediately set out for his home.

But before they had gone very far, the Centurion came out to meet them. "Lord, I am a man with authority and have soldiers under me," he explained. "I tell them to do something, to come or to go, and they do it. But I am not worthy for you to come into my house. Just say the word—and my servant will be healed."

Jesus looked at the Roman commander with amazement. In him, he saw a kindred spirit, a leader with great authority as well as great concern for those under him. Given the chance, this was someone He would have been good friends with.

"Truly, I tell you, I haven't seen faith like this in all Israel!" Jesus said to those who had followed Him. Then Jesus put one firm hand on the Centurion's shoulder and clasped his hand with the other, one leader to another. "Go back home. What you believed will be done for you."

And the servant was healed that same hour.

The Centurion in this story is known first and foremost, not for his great accomplishments, but for his great love and commitment to those under his authority. Rather than contempt, he has shown consideration for the Jewish community. Over the years, he has led, not by intimidation, but by building trust and respect. Now we see his concern for a servant who is desperately ill. It is clear that his first priority is the welfare of those he oversees. Why is this type of leader so rare?

Kris Kristofferson, who initially worked as a janitor at Columbia Records Studio where Johnny recorded, has said: "John was my hero a long time before I ever met him. He represented so much that appealed to me. He was willing and able to be the champion of people who didn't have one."

Emmylou Harris noted, "He seemed to be the voice of truth in everything he did. There was nothing unnatural about John Cash—this was not an act."

A Reprise Records release summarized his achievement this way: "Johnny Cash has had many imitators, The only 'real deal' of course has been Johnny Cash himself, real and unretouched."

When asked to comment after Johnny's death, Bob Dylan said of him, "Johnny was and is the North Star. You could guide your ship by him."

Merle Haggard, who was an inmate at San Quentin Prison when Johnny played there on New Year's Day in 1958, has stated, "He was like Abraham or Moses—one of the great men who will ever grace the earth."

Chance Martin, John's longtime friend, claimed that Johnny Cash was born to be special. "Johnny related to people," Martin remembered. "I've seen him pray for people. He was always kind and giving. I knew Johnny, but I needed to know Jesus Christ—and Johnny Cash made sure of that."

Perhaps Bono put it best when he said, "Every man could relate to him, but nobody could be him. To be that extraordinary and that ordinary was his real gift."

To be a high-ranking officer in the Roman army during the time of Rome's greatness could have been a reason for pride. Those with such status—whether in rank or worldly fame—are rarely humble. When given a prestigious title or celebrity, people often come to see themselves as more important than those who are under them. And yet rather than needing to make it clear who he is and what place he holds in the empire, the Centurion tells Jesus, "I am not worthy to receive you."

Anne Graham Lotz described the way that the King of Kings and Leader of Leaders was able to transform John's life: "God can take somebody whose life is like Johnny Cash's, put his spirit in him, and use him for his glory."

Carl Perkins called Johnny a "solid rock in this quicksand world" and told him, "You've been a friend with a heart as big as you are, a helping hand to all mankind."

Throughout his life, Johnny Cash recognized something about himself that many people with his kind of fame fail to see, *but for the grace of God, he too would be among the downcast and downtrodden.*

In a 1973 interview Johnny did for *Country Music*, he talked about the source of real fulfillment in life. "There's preaching Christians, church-playing Christians, and there's practicing Christians," he said. "And I'm trying very hard to be a practicing Christian. If you take the words of Jesus literally and apply them to your everyday life, you discover that the greatest fulfillment you'll ever find really does lie in giving."

CHAPTER 7

Calm in the Storm

THEY HAD SAILED HUNDREDS OF times on Galilee, a lake known for its storms. But this time as the waves broke over the sides of the boat and threatened to sink it in the inky depths, they feared for their lives.

They had spent a long day with Jesus as He taught the crowds about the kingdom of heaven and told how faith the size of a tiny mustard seed can grow to be very large.

When evening came, Jesus was tired and needed to rest. Most of all, He needed time away from the crowds. "Let us go over to the other side," He said to his apostles. And climbing into their boat, he curled up on a cushion and immediately fell asleep.

"We must wake the Master! Before it's too late!" one of them suggested, and everyone agreed.

"Teacher! Teacher!" they called, their shouts carried

away by the wind. "Master!" the disciples cried again, louder this time. "Master! Don't you care if we drown?"

Shaking off His sleep, Jesus got on His feet and surveyed the chaotic scene. Then turning to the crashing waves, He raised His hands and called out in a voice of authority, "Peace! Be still!" Immediately the wind and the seas calmed.

In the hushed silence, Jesus turned back to His disciples and simply said, "Oh you of little faith"—words which suggested they had much more to learn and yet at the same time acknowledged they did have something, something small like the mustard seed.

"What kind of man is this that even the winds and waves obey him?" the apostles whispered to themselves. Christ's ability to command the storm with just three words showed His authority over all of creation and revealed that He truly was God.

"There's a storm coming at Bon Aqua, a big one that's blown all the way from the Pacific."

With these words, Johnny opens chapter three of the Bon Aqua section of his autobiography. He goes on to tell readers, "I'm sitting in my library, looking out the westward-facing window at the strengthening rain and the blackening sky."

With the strong frame of the farmhouse around him, a structure that had weathered storms since before the Civil War, Cash reports that he felt safe and secure.

"Such moments are open invitations to closeness with God," Cash concludes. "Nature at work isn't itself God, but it is evidence of Him, and by letting myself be drawn into its depths and intrigues, I can come near to Him, see the glory of His creation, feel the salve of His grace."

Late in life, during his time working with Rick Rubin, as John faced the storms of aging, increasing illness, and the approach of death, he recorded "You'll Never Walk Alone"—the classic show tune from *Carousel*, the beloved 1945 musical by Rodgers and Hammerstein. The track would appear on the box set *Unearthed*, released in 2003, two months after his death.

As he sings with a voice weakened by time but strong in faith, Johnny reminds each of us to never give up hope because on the other side of every storm waits a golden sky.

> When you walk through a storm,
> Hold your head up high
> And don't be afraid of the dark.
> At the end of the storm
> There's a golden sky
> And the sweet silver song of the lark.
>
> Walk on, through the wind,
> Walk on, through the rain,
> Though your dreams be tossed and blown.
> Walk on, walk on, with hope in your heart
> And you'll never walk alone.
> You'll never walk alone.

CHAPTER 8

Mercy

ACCUSED OF ADULTERY, SHE STOOD in shame before everyone. The crowd taunted her with insults. Some were starting to pick up rocks. Suddenly a voice cried, "Teacher, the law of Moses commands us to stone such women. What do you say?"

The crowd grew silent. Only now did the woman raise her head enough to see the man the question had been directed to. Standing by Himself off to the side, there was something special about Him, a stillness that could not be disturbed. Slowly and deliberately He looked at each face of those so eager to harm her. Then without saying a word, He slowly stooped and began writing on the ground.

"Didn't you hear me?" said the big man who had spoken. "I asked you what we should do with this Jezebel."

As though He had all the time in the world, the man stopped writing and slowly stood up. In a quiet voice that echoed off the temple walls, the calm man finally answered.

"I say that if any one of you is without sin, let him be the first one to throw a stone." Then He stooped again and continued his writing.

The woman dropped her head, squeezed her eyes shut, and waited for the barrage that would end her life. Seconds ticked by. Then more. Then one by one, she heard the sound of rocks being dropped and feet shuffling off. Finally, all was quiet again. Then she heard footsteps, deliberate, unhurried steps coming toward her.

"Where are your accusers?" the quiet voice asked. A calloused hand with a tender touch gently raised her head. The woman opened her eyes and looking into His found not scorn but a compassion she had never known. For the second time that day she thought she was going to die—this time from being loved like that.

"Has no one condemned you?" the man of love asked again.

Looking around at the empty courtyard, she answered, "No one, Sir."

"Then neither do I condemn you. Go now and leave your life of sin."

I was asked how my grandfather showed mercy. I've been asked a lot of things, but not that one. Immediately a scene popped into my head.

During the last few years of my grandpa's life, I was deep into my own addiction which was similar to his. With a half-gallon of vodka a day, Xanax, cocaine, and amphetamines, it was not exactly in the closet.

During this time, I stole from him—some rather sentimental items. Not that that matters, it could have been anything. The fact is I stole from the man who had been there for me and who loved me. My own flesh and blood.

He knew it and confronted me. To stand before him and admit (which in my cowardice I would not have done on my own) that I had taken from him—I don't remember a lot of that period of time, but I'll never forget that.

"I guess you needed it more than I did," is what he said.

How do you answer that?

I didn't answer; honestly, I don't know what I did. I'm sure it was just as pathetic as how I felt. I don't remember. What I do remember is he never raised his voice, he never belittled me, he not once showed anger. He showed pain and disappointment. I'll always feel remnants of that moment. A scar I'm now grateful for. But he knew, he understood where I was—the abyss of addiction that I was in. He had been in that hell of his own creation. He knew it was not Thomas that was standing in front of him. He knew.

So, he offered me help. He wanted me back.

I am very sad to say he didn't get that from me. He never saw me sober again. It took another 13 years for that to happen. This incident happened the winter before he passed.

So to answer the question, "How did your grandfather show mercy?"—that is my answer.

CHAPTER 9

Blind But Now I See

THE GOSPEL OF JOHN, CHAPTER 9, begins by telling us of a man who had been blind from birth. Six verses later John reports that after his encounter with Jesus this same man came home seeing.

It boggles the mind.

To have left home that day, never having seen anything—not a blade of grass, a leaf on a tree, or a cloud in the sky, not his own family, not even his own face—and to go to bed that night having seen hundreds of things that at breakfast he had only heard people talk about was amazing.

Imagine this man walking home through the crowded streets, a strange look on his face, turning his head this way and that, not wanting to miss anything. Imagine people who had seen him all his life having to fumble and grope his way around town, now asking each other in astonishment, "Isn't this the blind man who used to sit in the market every day and beg?"

"It can't be him!" some said. "It must be someone who looks like him!" others claimed.

The Pharisees insisted on questioning the man about the One who had cured his blindness. They had already decided that anyone who acknowledged that Jesus was the Christ would immediately be put out of the synagogue. "We know that this man who healed you is a sinner," they said. "What have you to say about it?"

"Whether he is a sinner or not, I don't know. One thing I do know—I was blind but now I see!"

Johnny Cash would often perform Hank Williams' great song of faith "I Saw the Light." And when he did, he sometimes added a new verse he had written that described his own story.

In it he tells of a time when he was like the blind man in the Gospel, wandering alone in darkness, full of worries and fears. But then, like the blind man whose sight was miraculously restored by Jesus, Cash reports, "Praise the Lord, I saw the light."

One of the things fans liked most about Johnny Cash was his honesty. For example, he made no secret of the fact that his life was a mixture of a darkness blacker than midnight and a light strong enough to pierce the darkness. Toward the end of his life, he fought a different kind of darkness as his eyesight began to fail and he needed someone to read to him. In many cases this person was his daughter Cindy.

In 2003, he asked Cindy to take him out to the farm for one last look. Sensing the end was not far off, he made her a present of the collection of glass bottles that had sat in the Bon Aqua kitchen window for the past thirty years. Then he went into the library he had loved and sat at his desk where he thumbed through a few books. Unable to make out the words anymore, he soon grew frustrated and before long he was ready to leave. He had said his goodbye. Eight months later he made the ultimate journey.

THE CAGE

Though every day more feeble,
he still could shake the cage.
Through a daughter's eyes he read the Book,
his own made weak by age.

Confined now to a wheelchair,
he had a guarantee
from the One who made the lame to walk
and caused the blind to see.

He left with just a whisper
instead of with a roar.
But when he reached the other side,
he crashed through Heaven's door.

Now he runs upon the rainbow,
and all his chains are gone.
He can see the farthest galaxy
and dance beyond the dawn.

As he joined the new creation,
he let his praises soar.
Though broken down in this world,
he crashed through Heaven's door.

CHAPTER 10

Man of Sorrows, Man in Black

JOHN, CHAPTER 11, BEGINS WITH seven words: "Now a man named Lazarus was sick."

Lazarus was a common name at the time—so common that Jesus used it in His parable about the poor beggar who sat at the rich man's gate. But this Lazarus was the brother of Mary and Martha, and these siblings were three of His best friends.

The sisters kept vigil as their brother's condition worsened. Finally, they sent a message that simply said, "Lord, the one you love is sick."

There is a feeling of dread that comes with this kind of message where we read between the lines and understand that this person might not make it, and that if we don't come soon, we may not see them alive.

Jesus was out of town when He got the news. But rather than adjusting His plans so He could go visit this friend that He loved, Jesus decided to stay where He was for two more days. The disciples must have been surprised at His decision, but the only explanation He offered was that God would be glorified through this illness.

Mary and Martha were confused and hurt by the delay. By the time Jesus arrived, their brother was dead. The first thing they said was, "If only you had been here…" And in these words, Jesus heard their deep sorrow and their huge loss. And as the sisters wept, we are told Jesus wept with them.

Jesus wept. The shortest verse in the King James Bible. Profoundly simple, but packed with immeasurable love. Witnessing the grief of this family and their friends, Jesus shares their grief.

Jesus wept—he felt real sadness and really wept. And so Isaiah's prophecy about the coming Messiah was fulfilled: *He was a man of sorrows and acquainted with grief.*

On February 17, 1971, *The Johnny Cash Show* aired a special-themed episode called "Johnny Cash on Campus." The climax of the evening came when Johnny introduced a brand-new song he had written after a series of discussions with Vanderbilt students about challenges the country was facing.

"This song is a very personal thing," he stated—suggesting that while all his songs were personal, this one came from a place where his deepest feelings were kept. "It's the way I feel about a lot of things."

Then using cue cards to follow the words because he had not had time to memorize them yet, Johnny Cash debuted what would be his signature song for the rest of his life, "The Man in Black."

On that cold February night, if anyone had wondered why Johnny Cash always dressed in black, they learned that he did so as a reminder to those who were more fortunate in life that there were others who were poor and beaten down who lived lives of hopelessness.

The audience in the Ryman Auditorium that evening learned that John wore black for the prisoners who had paid for their crimes but were still in jail. He wore black so that those who were doing fine would always be reminded of the lonely, the elderly, the veterans, and the junkies on the street and the lives that might have been.

Johnny Cash wore black to remind us all that for many people, things were far from okay, and that until things got brighter for everyone, he would try, as he put it, to carry off a little darkness on his back.

Until that day, he would be the Man in Black.

CHAPTER 11

Let the Children Come

CHRISTIANS TODAY OFTEN FORGET HOW popular Jesus was with the lowly and downtrodden. He kept a special place in His heart for these people others looked down on.

They came from near and far to hear Him talk about a kingdom where the meek and the poor in spirit are called blessed. How they loved to sit at His feet and listen to stories about His Father who cared for each of them, like a good shepherd cares for his sheep.

As Jesus' fame grew—and with it the crowds—His disciples did not understand that He was not going to be like the other leaders of the world. He wasn't going to build a following of high-ranking movers and shakers. From His beginnings in a humble stable to His friendships with prostitutes and tax collectors, Jesus had a different way of doing things.

Look at the disciples in the picture. See their frustration and anger as they try to hold back the flood of pure joy that is breaking through the barriers they have set up. Imagine what they must be saying and the tone they must be using.

Hey, you, get back here! The Master can't be bothered with children! He doesn't have time for you! The Master has much more important things to do than to hang out with a bunch of kids!

Now look at Jesus. See His outstretched hands. See His complete focus on the little child racing toward Him. He is so happy to see her, He can hardly wait.

Finally, look at the children's faces filled to the brim with gladness. They are running as fast as their feet can go, and nothing is going to stop them because they know something the disciples don't.

They know that nothing in the world is more important to Jesus than they are.

If the farm at Bon Aqua was a place where Johnny Cash could go to truly be alone, it was also a place where he could go to truly spend time with his children in a way not possible elsewhere.

Cindy Cash explains that at the farm she saw the fun and mischievous side of her father. "He taught me how to shoot a gun there," she notes. "And how to bait a hook and find arrowheads."

In the quiet and solitude of the farm, Cindy was able to rediscover her father and know that he loved her without reservation. For this reason she has described it as "the most sentimental place in the world to me."

Tara Cash, the youngest of the sisters, remembers all of them climbing into the Jeep and setting off across the property to search for arrowheads. As they drove, they would sing "Children, Go Where I Send Thee" with each one taking a turn singing a verse.

"I remember having lots of people on the porch," Tara recalls. "And even though it may or may not have been the fourth of July, Dad would churn ice cream, and we'd eat watermelon and shoot off fireworks."

In an essay she wrote for *Oxford American*, Rosanne Cash tells how she and her sisters spent part of every summer at Bon Aqua picking wild blackberries, playing music on the porch, and sneaking off to visit the county psychic.

In a moving passage she describes how her father would make peach ice cream out in the yard with fruit from their own trees, and would crank the old-fashioned ice cream maker until his arm ached but would never complain. She shares the story of how he rented the entire skating rink so they could skate in private because when her father was with them in public they never had a moment of peace.

Rosanne tells readers that these times spent with her father were pure and healing, and that during those years love grew of its own accord.

CHAPTER 12

Confronting the Moneychangers

"**Your weights must be wrong!**" Jesus heard an old man exclaim. "My coins are worth more than that!"

"But there is no blemish on the animal I brought to sacrifice," cried another man at an animal stall across the courtyard. "Why should I have to buy another one? And at twice the ordinary cost!"

"Is this the holy place we came all this way to pray in?" a young boy asked his father, confusion and fear in his voice. "How can we pray to God here? It's so noisy. And everything smells like manure."

Jesus had seen the sorry sight before. The greedy moneychangers who cheated the poor Jews from the provinces who needed to exchange their foreign coins for Jewish shekels, the only currency accepted for paying the temple tax. The corrupt priests who rejected perfectly fine animals brought from outside, so those wishing to make a sacrifice had to purchase one at double the price from temple sellers who shared their profits with the priests.

The Passover—the holiest day in the Jewish calendar—had become a day of moneymaking. And the once sacred courtyard of the Temple, a place intended for prayer and reciting the holy texts, had been turned into a stockyard filled with excrement.

How can we pray to God here? The boy's words echoed in His mind as Jesus thought back when He had first come as a boy with His parents to the Temple. Then He made His decision. Striding over to the table where the first man stood, Jesus reached down and took one of the weights off the scale and broke it apart. It was made of clay!

"You would cheat the elderly in the house of God?" Jesus said with righteous anger. And then with arms made strong by years of hauling timber and sawing wood, He grabbed the edge of the table and flipped it over like a twig, sending coins flying everywhere.

As the crooked moneychanger raced after his money, Jesus went from one table to the next, turning each one over in succession. "It is written," He cried in a voice that filled the courtyard, "My house will be called a house of prayer, but you have made it a den of robbers!"

Then Jesus moved to the area where the cattle and sheep were being sold. Cracking a whip, He sent the livestock out of the Temple. Finally, He marched over to the dove cages and set every bird free.

"Take your tethers, and cages, and cashboxes, and get out!" He yelled to the ones who had been selling the animals. "How dare you turn my Father's house into a market!"

No one dared stop Him. In fact, most people were thrilled someone had taken a stand against the corruption. His plain robes, His Galilean accent, and His workingman strength told them this was no Sadducee or Pharisee. This man was one of them.

For years, the holy space had been desecrated. But now it was cleansed and ready once more for the purpose God had intended—to be a house of prayer.

In October 1980, Waylon Jennings and his wife Jessi Colter were spending time at Johnny's Bon Aqua farm. John used the opportunity to record an interview with his old friend for a piece that became the cover story of the April 1981 issue of *Country Music* magazine.

"The old log house was cool and quiet," Cash begins. "The one hundred acres of pastures and woods around it were alive with the chattering of wild birds. Waylon was asleep on the couch."

In their conversation, Cash and Jennings got talking about their need to have time away from the business of making music. "You know what getting away from it all is for me?" Cash confessed. "This place here."

Soon their conversation turned to the executives who controlled the music business and the troubled relationships that they both had with them.

"Speaking of trust," Johnny asked, "how far do you trust record company executives?"

"Is there any way you can?" Waylon asked. "How long will it be before you can trust one? That should be the question. I look at record companies and corporations—the thing is, there's no human element there. They're paid to do a job. They're paid to take care of business for the record company. That's one of the main problems that I always had dealing with a record company."

The older Johnny Cash grew, the more he came to resent the music executives and the country-music establishment who had abandoned him and the other aging country artists who had once defined the genre. Country radio came to have less and less room for Johnny's music on their playlists, and finally no room at all.

When *Unchained*, which had been ignored by the country-music establishment, won a Grammy for Best Country Album, Cash and his producers posted an advertisement in the March 14, 1998 issue of *Billboard Magazine*. It featured the now famous photo of Cash giving the finger to the camera, along with these words: "American Recordings and Johnny Cash would like to acknowledge the Nashville music establishment and country radio for your support."

In Cash's gesture he was making a statement to the music industry and music executives not only for himself but also for all the marginalized country performers who were thought to be past their prime. "Yes, we may be older now, but we are still artists. We still have worth. We still have music to make and things to say. And we can still win awards."

CHAPTER 13

Gifts from the Heart

A CROWD WAS GATHERED IN THE temple treasury. Some of Jerusalem's wealthiest businessmen were going to give their offerings! First they had to decide how much to put into each of the receptacles located around the room. Each container had a different purpose—this one to buy wood, that one for sacrifices, this one for incense, and so on.

After making their decision, the rich men would take out their heavy coins. Sometimes they would drop them one by one. Sometimes they would pour in an entire bag. The crowd oohed and aahed as the coins clinked and clanked. After an especially large gift, they would break into applause.

The Gospel writers tell us that many wealthy people gave a great deal that day. But the story they go on to relate is not about large amounts of money or someone doing anything remarkable in the world's eyes. In fact, according to human standards, what they tell about was one of the least noteworthy events recorded in the entire New Testament.

Unnoticed by everyone, a poor widow joined the line. When it came her turn, she stepped up to the coffer and placed in her offering—two very small coins worth only a fraction of a penny. A seemingly insignificant contribution, they made no sound as they hit the sides and slid to the bottom. Still unnoticed, the woman disappeared back into the crowd.

But Jesus was close enough to see the wrinkled hand and the two small coins. He alone knew what this gift had cost her. "Truly I say to you," Jesus told the disciples who were with Him, "this poor widow has put in more than all these others. They gave out of their abundance. She has put in all she had to live on."

Though the actual amount the poor widow gave was insignificant, her story lives on as one of the Bible's best known illustrations of generosity and trust. Given the size of the temple and the cost of its upkeep, by the world's standards her gift was inconsequential. But while man judges by quantity, the smallest gift of the poor is of infinite value to God.

The poor widow knew something that we often forget. She knew that giving is a privilege and a blessing. She also knew God would provide for her that day, and the day after as well. Rather than putting her trust in her savings account, she put her confidence in God and knew He would never fail her.

Of all those who came to make their offering that day, the poor widow was the richest in faith.

DECEMBER 20, 1984

COMPASSION SHOWN, HUMILITY TAUGHT
by Cindy Cash

I had some issues going on in my life and was staying with my dad. I was about 24 years old. One morning, my dad came in my room and woke me. He said, "Hey! Come ride with me to take John Carter (my brother) to school." He was about 14.

On the way back home, we were riding along talking and looking at the snow outside. It was pretty cold that day. As we drove by a bridge, we could see a man underneath it rolling up a sleeping bag as though he had just woken up.

Dad pulled over. There we were in his long, black Mercedes, pulling onto the gravel under the bridge approaching what appeared to be a homeless man in this freezing weather packing up his bed.

Dad stopped the car and turned to me. "Stay here."

Well, no way was I going to miss this. I quietly got out of my side of the car and tiptoed closer so I could hear.

DAD: "Hi, Son. Where you headed?"

MAN: "Just hitchhiking up to Kentucky to spend Christmas with my wife and kids."

DAD: "Where you coming from?"

MAN: "Florida. Hey! You're Johnny Cash, aren't you?"

DAD: *(reaching out his hand)* "I'm John. What's your name?"

MAN: "My name's Jason."

DAD: "Isn't it a little cold to be hitchhiking? How long has it taken you to get to Tennessee from Florida?"

JASON: "Three days."

DAD: *(reaching in his pocket)* "Well, here's some bus fare. And a little extra to buy your wife and kids some Christmas gifts. Merry Christmas."

JASON: "Hey, man! This is $1,000!"

DAD: "Just don't forget to buy those babies some presents."

Dad got back in the car closing the door only seconds after me.

HE SAID: "Cindy, I told you to stay in the car."

I SAID: "Dad, that was so sweet of you." I was crying.

He put the car in reverse, looked over at me, put his finger to his lips, and simply said, "Shhh…."

JOHNNY'S SECRET GIFT
by Tommy Cash

I toured with Johnny a whole year in 1976, and we worked 121 concerts. We were at the University of Wisconsin one night in '76, and we were in the dressing room which was the men's locker room for the basketball team. And I saw Johnny walking up and down the aisles in the dressing room looking into the lockers with the little square holes.

I said, "What are you doing?"

And he said, "Nothing."

I said, "What are you looking in the lockers for?"

He said, "Well, I'm looking for the ball player that has the oldest worn-out tennis shoes and gym shorts."

I watched him, and I saw him roll up a hundred-dollar bill and stick it through one of those squares and drop it in this kid's tennis shoes.

And I said, "John, that absolutely amazes me that you would do that."

And he said, "Can you imagine when that kid comes to basketball practice on Monday? And he'll always wonder where that $100 bill came from."

CHAPTER 14

In the Garden

JESUS LOOKED DOWN AT THE sleeping disciples. Except for their beards and weather-beaten faces, Peter and John almost looked like two young boys after a long day.

On this evening in particular, Jesus had hoped these special two would have stayed awake with Him to pray, to offer a word of encouragement, or just to be with Him. But the grueling schedule had taken its toll. First one and then the other had dropped off, leaving Him alone.

He, too, was weary—weary to His bones, but Jesus knew He would not sleep this night.

He alone grasped what was to come. He alone foresaw the suffering it would be His part to bear. He walked deeper into the garden, through the shifting patterns of moonlight and shadow. And then He fell to his knees, turning to His Heavenly Father as He had so many times before.

"If it's possible," Jesus began, His heart full of agony.

"If it's possible!" He pleaded as He wrestled with fear and became drenched in sweat.

"If it's possible," He cried out, "let this cup pass from me."

Then there came something from within Him, deep beneath the anguish. And He found the steadfastness that had been there throughout His ministry. He did not feel fearless or particularly courageous, but knew this did not matter. He had found the answer He was searching for.

"But not as I will, but as you will."

Jesus raised His head and wiped the sweat from His eyes. Far off in the distance, He saw the torches beginning to make their way up the hill toward Him—the priests and soldiers led by Judas, who was coming to betray Him. Once more the terror overcame Him. And gradually once more, below the torment and dread, He found the determination to finish the job He had come to do.

"Not as I will," He said once more, a fierce light in his eyes. "but as you will." Then Jesus got to His feet and woke the sleeping apostles.

"The hour has come," He said, fully ready and fully willing to face what was to come.

LAST TRIP TO BON AQUA

When *Cash: The Autobiography* was released in 1997, Johnny Cash had already owned the farm at Bon Aqua for twenty-five years. And in those twenty-five years it had become an inseparable part of his life.

John begins the Bon Aqua section of his autobiography with the report that immediately after getting home from a tour that had taken him to some of the world's greatest cities, he packed a small suitcase and went out to the farm by himself for a few days of, as he puts it, just pottering about.

"This is a great place for pottering," Cash explains. "I can cook my own food, read my own books, tend my own garden, wander my own land. I can think, write, compose, study, rest, and reflect in peace."

"Saturday Night in Hickman County" was written at Bon Aqua. And it was here that Cash wrote "I'm Gonna Sit on the Porch and Pick on My Old Guitar." When it came time to film his first Christmas special, Johnny asked Roy Clark and Tony Orlando, two of the biggest names in the business, to shoot the opening segments at the farm with him.

And yet, it was the simple, daily routine that Cash had at the farm that meant the most to him. He tells readers, "I like to dig in the dirt. I like to work in the fields and the garden. I come up here and I wear a cap or an old straw hat."

In an interview, Johnny spoke with biographer Steve Turner about the little spring that was located at the back of the farm. And in his comments, we can hear hints of what it was that he found there.

"I like to get up there and drink from that spring," Cash told Turner. "I just lay on the ground beside it. That's paradise on earth to me, that little place with the dogwood and sycamore trees all around. You don't hear a car, a train, a plane, or anything. All you can hear is nature."

In 2003, just months before his death, Johnny Cash asked his daughter Cindy to drive him to the farm for one last visit to the place that he called the center of his universe. Here is how Cindy Cash described that last trip.

I took Dad to the farm the last time he was there. It was prior to June's death. Approximately seven or eight months before his own passing, he could still walk, but his eyesight was failing.

He gave me all the glass bottles that had sat in the same kitchen window for thirty years.

He sat down at his desk and asked me to bring him a Coke. He thumbed through a few books, but I knew he was getting frustrated at the fact that he couldn't see anymore.

Finally, he stopped trying to read and started writing. I just let him be until he needed something.

I could tell he was saying goodbye to the farm, and it broke my heart forever.

This was to be Johnny's last time to be at the farm he loved so much. Eight months later on September 12, 2003, he made the ultimate journey.

CHAPTER 15

Two Opposite Kinds of Shame

TODAY, CROSSES ARE A COMMON sight. We see them on church steeples and inside sanctuaries in places of honor. In cemeteries everywhere, elaborate memorials with crosses pay tribute to our beloved ones who have died.

But in the world of the New Testament, a cross conveyed only one message: Shame. Slaves, rebels convicted of treason, murderers, and the vilest criminals were crucified on crosses. Crucifixion was not just a way to bring a slow and agonizing death. It was also a way to publicly and utterly shame someone.

The shame of the cross. This five-word phrase has been heard so often that it may lack any real meaning today as we fail to remember that the whole point of everything from the arrest to the crucifixion was for Jesus to be completely humiliated.

Those who struck Him or spit on Him and mocked Him, those who had Him flogged or put a crown of thorns on His head, those who gambled for His only garment, and those who nailed Him to a cross—this was their goal: To leave Jesus disgraced, exposed, and completely powerless. And yet Christ freely accepted this shame for us.

Look at the faces of those who gather at the foot of the cross. On one side, John and Mary stand filled with horror but refusing to abandon our Lord in His greatest need. They share in and are present in Christ's shame. On the other side, see the jeering Roman soldier who finds pleasure in insulting Jesus. Next to him stands the chief priest, his arms crossed and a smug look of satisfaction on his face. Somehow in his twisted, self-important sense of piety, he has convinced himself that helping to bring about Jesus' shame was a way for him to serve God.

What would your reaction have been to the utter shame of Jesus, the shame of Him who knew no guilt?

"THE DARKNESS FROM THE GUILT"
by Cindy Cash

Two weeks were up. He still wasn't home. Mom waited. And waited. And started the phone calls. No word. Nothing.

Two months later, she went to see her doctor. "If you don't file for divorce, June will be raising your girls because you will be dead." That's all she heard. *June will be raising your girls.*

My mom would not have that. Maybe over her dead body. She waited until Friday. If the news flash came out on Saturday, her girls wouldn't be in school to hear the taunts from their friends: "Johnny Cash's wife files for divorce."

So she did.

She gathered her four girls and along with her friend, Carol, and her children they took off for a vacation to Crater Lake, Oregon. This way, her girls would be nowhere around to hear the news.

Home on Sunday, to school on Monday. Monday, late to the press, the front page read "Johnny Cash's wife files for divorce." She was devastated. All her efforts were of no use. Her girls were questioned only to answer they didn't know. "What's a divorce, Mama?"

On the other side, Dad was on the road still. No word from him as he was with June. They were on the road together when he was finally found by a court appointed server and told his wife had filed for divorce.

Anger. No longer in control. Now he knows. She knows. More anger. An overwhelming flow of emotion. He had just written "Ring of Fire."

I'll show her. I'll put June's and Merle's names as songwriters. She won't get these royalties. Done.... But my girls. When will I see my girls?

He simply couldn't take it. Total devastation. *What will they say? Who? Everyone! My parents. My fans. My God. Oh! My God.* The guilt overwhelmed him.

I have forsaken my God. I have broken a commandment. Thou shalt not commit adultery. I've made Vivian file for divorce. A Catholic sin at the worst. No more receiving of communion. She will be devastated. June, what did I do?

Well, he drove himself to a place called Nickajack Lake. Along the banks was a cave. He crawled inside this cave and decided if he continued to crawl until he could see no light, no more, nothing, he would die and everyone would be free of his pain, including him.

In his terrible shame, his faith had been challenged. "Yes, and it had lost," he thought. He crawled in and laid down to die. "I'm sorry, my Lord. Oh, poor me. Pitiful me…"

He felt a hand. He was being pulled from the cave. It was a sheriff.

He was in a jail cell. The sheriff said, "I sure do hate to have to go home and tell my wife who is in my jail. She loves your gospel songs."

Humility….

Who do you think you are that you can take your
own life and be selfish enough to hurt four little girls
that love you, a woman you brought the
depths of pain to, a God you disappointed?

You are no one. No one better than the other.
Humble yourself as like a little child….

Cindy Cash, December 2, 2017

CHAPTER 16

Mary Magdalene

POSSESSED! THAT'S WHAT THEY WHISPERED about the wild-eyed woman who stumbled around town mumbling to herself, her clothes and hair a dirty, disheveled mess. Tortured and tormented by unseen shadows, she was known to cut herself with stones and to throw herself into the fire or water.

But He had taken pity on her. He had called her by her name and had spoken words that had driven away the darkness and brought her into the light.

From that moment on, she had never left His side.

She had traveled with Him as He went from town to town, the crowds hanging on His every word. She had been there all during the shame of His so-called trial, even when the others fled.

She had listened as Pilate pronounced His sentence and had heard the religious leaders clamoring for His blood.

She had stood by Him as He was cursed and spat upon, and was made to wear a crown of thorns. She had fought to stay close as the jostling crowd had pushed Him up the hill where the nails were driven into His hands and feet.

She had stayed there all during His slow, unbearable death and had finally heard Him cry, "It is finished!" Then as dusk fell, she had helped take His cold, lifeless body from the cross and bring it to the tomb.

Then had come the Sabbath—a day of shock and dreadful numbness. A day of waiting, waiting for Sunday to come when she could return.

In the pale light before daybreak she had risen and had hurried alone through the silent streets. Carrying her packet of spices, she had come to the garden on the outskirts of town, hoping to do what little was left—to anoint His dead body and say her final farewell, a last act of gratitude to the One who had made her whole again.

But when she had arrived, the tomb was empty, the corpse was gone. *Why would anyone take a dead body?* It made no sense. But nothing in the past four days made sense. She sunk to the ground and wept—finally letting down the brave front she had kept up for Him. As the sobs took over her, she thought back to the time He had gone with her into the shadows. Now she felt the darkness gathering around her again.

"Woman," said a voice nearby, probably just the gardener come to work, "why do you weep?"

Unable to raise her head, she struggled to get the words out. "They have taken my Lord away, and I don't know where they have put him." Then desperation gave her the courage to add, "Sir, if you have carried him away, tell me where you have put him."

They have taken my Lord away.... My Lord. My Own. My Dear One.

And then came one word from a voice she recognized, calling her name again like when it had driven the darkness away.

"Mary."

Gazing up into the brightness, she saw the gentle smile she knew so well and looked into the eyes she most wanted to see—eyes full of love and alive once more. *Alive!* The word ran through her—at first like a trickle after winter's first thaw and then like a mighty torrent. *Alive!*

"Teacher!" was all she could manage to say as she fell at His feet bathed in heavenly light. *Alive!*

In 1971, Johnny Cash began filming *The Gospel Road*, a ninety-minute movie about the life of Christ shot on location in Israel. Reba, Johnny's sister, played the Virgin Mary. And June played Mary Magdalene.

John saw *The Gospel Road* as a part of his ministry, and though it never made a big splash at the box office, he and June would later call it some of their "proudest work."

John opens the scene where Jesus heals Mary Magdalene by telling viewers: "The scriptures don't tell a lot about her, but what little is told has made her the subject of more speculation and controversy than any woman I ever heard of."

He goes on to state, "Jesus was to suffer much criticism for his association with people of questionable character. 'He dines with publicans and sinners!' they said. And to that Jesus replied, 'It's the sick that need a physician, not the healthy.'

And this woman needed him.... Mary was the kind of woman that Jesus was to have a lot of love and compassion for, a lot of love and compassion."

And so it was not Peter or John, and not even his mother, Mary, that the Risen Lord chose to reveal Himself to first. It was the former outcast, Mary Magdalene.

Why Mary Magdalene? Perhaps because more so than these others, she had once been despised and rejected, and was from "the least of these"—the very people the great physician came to heal.

CHAPTER 17

A Shepherd's Heart

PETER RUBBED HIS EYES. It had been a long night. Five of them had gone back to Tiberias and had taken the boat out of its moorings and had gone fishing on the Sea of Galilee.

What else was there to do?

But they had caught absolutely nothing. A long, exasperating night of casting the heavy net, watching it sink, hauling it in, and finding it empty. Now in the cold hour before dawn, they were headed back with nothing but weary hearts and weary arms.

This was my idea, thought Peter. Well, anything was better than another sleepless night remembering his failure.

"Lord, why can't I follow you now? I will lay down my life for you!" That's what he had told the Master after

Judas had gone out. "Even if all the others fall away, I never will."

Empty promises from an empty-headed fool.

"Hey, you there, by the fire! Aren't you one of his disciples?" That's what they had asked him.

"I tell you I don't know him!" He had replied, not once but several times. And the final time, the Lord, who was bound and standing with the soldiers, had turned and looked straight at him. Three denials before the rooster crowed. Three chances to declare his allegiance to Jesus. Three failures just as the Master had predicted.

If only I could do it all over…. If only I could have another chance….

"Friends, have you caught anything?" A voice from the shore roused Peter from his thoughts. "Throw your net on the right side and you will find fish." They did, and when they tried to pull it in, the net was too full to lift.

"It's the Lord!" cried John turning to Peter. But Peter was already in the sea, swimming toward the Master as fast as he could.

Jesus motioned the dripping apostle to join Him by the fire where fish were roasting over the glowing coals. "Come and have some breakfast." After they had all eaten, Peter knew he must try to somehow take back the words he had said. But the Master spoke first.

"Simon, son of John, do you love me?" Three times, Jesus—the Great Physician and Healer of Souls—asked Peter this question. Three times Peter was given the chance to profess his love and reverse his previous failure. "Yes, Lord, you know that I love you." And after three times, Jesus reassigned Peter the task he had been given from the start: "Feed my sheep."

Feed my sheep. Lead and protect my flock after I am gone. Care for the elderly ones whose strength is failing. Watch over the young lambs who need your wisdom. Seek out those sheep who are lost and bring them safely back to the fold.

And fully restored and fully forgiven, this is exactly what Peter did—with the heart of a shepherd.

Maverick. American Icon. Champion of the Poor and the Down-and-Out. Member of both the Country Music Hall of Fame and the Rock and Roll Hall of Fame. Television Show Host. Friend. Brother. Husband. Father. Grandfather. Man of God. Man in Black.

Johnny Cash was all of these and more. But beneath each of these titles he acquired later in life was one that he carried with him from his humble beginnings in the American South, a part of his identity that was always with him no matter what came later.

Johnny Cash was first, last, and always a country boy, and was most at home in pastures, barns, and fields.

He was a country boy in his love for the simple things in life—homemade food, fishing and hunting, a summer's day, having time for family and friends, going barefoot. A country boy in his love of being free—free from contracts, commitments, and ringing telephones.

And perhaps most of all, Johnny was a country boy in his love and his deep connection to the land and its Creator.

In 1950, when he was eighteen, Johnny Cash enlisted in the Air Force and left behind the rural cotton fields of Dyess, Arkansas. Thus began a twenty-two year journey that took him to live in

Europe, Memphis, California, and Nashville, and tours everywhere in between.

Then in 1972, he finally found a place in the gently rolling hills forty miles west of Nashville where he could come back to the land: A 100-acre farm called Bon Aqua.

It was a place where he could be Johnny Cash, Country Boy.

CHAPTER 18

Road to Damascus

THE SON OF WEALTHY PARENTS from the tribe of Benjamin. Born in the region's most prestigious city. The brightest pupil in their synagogue. Admitted to the legendary rabbinical school in Jerusalem to study under the great Gamaliel.

Saul of Tarsus was all these things. And now the Chief Priests had demonstrated their confidence in him. In his bag were letters with their seal authorizing him to arrest anyone, man or woman, belonging to the new heretical sect that was proclaiming that the Messiah had come.

Blasphemy! Didn't they know that when He came, Israel's Promised One would reveal Himself to the High Priest and the other members of the ruling class—not to a bunch of illiterate fishermen and tax collectors?

In his mind Saul rehearsed the moment when he would give the order and the armed men under his command would seize the heretics. He thought of the approval he would receive when he brought them bound like criminals to Jerusalem. Some would surely be put to death, and the sooner the world was cleansed of these people and their sacrilege, the better.

The closer they came to Damascus, the firmer Saul's resolution grew. He would show how tough he could be when it came to dealing with this troublesome cult.

Suddenly, a bright light poured from the heavens with the power of a great river forcing him to the ground. His heart pounded with terror, and he struggled for breath. Then came a Voice that knocked him flat on his face.

"Saul! Saul! Why do you persecute me?"

Unable to see in the blinding light, Saul struggled to raise his head and answer the Golden Radiance.

"Who are you, Lord?"

Out of the brilliant light came the answer that would change the course of his life.

"I am Jesus of Nazareth, whom you are persecuting."

In the silence that followed, scenes from his past came before him. And with each one, it became clearer that his entire life had been completely and horribly misguided.

In the Divine Righteousness that poured from the light, his own self-righteousness felt like a dirty rag that could no longer cover him. In shame and despair, he managed to stammer: "What shall I do, Lord?"

Then from the light there came not only judgment, but something that surprised him more than anything else that had happened that day—boundless love and unfathomable mercy.

"Get up, and go into Damascus," said the Voice. "There you will be told all that you have been assigned to do."

Struck blind, Saul was led by the hand into the city. Three days later he was baptized into the new religion he had previously tried to stamp out. Much later, his name changed to Paul, he wrote words that would encourage countless others: "Jesus came into the world to save sinners of whom I am chief."

Paul's vision of the Risen Lord transformed him into one of the most influential people in history. Johnny Cash's vision was of a very different man—his recently deceased father. This vision, which came to him in a dream, helped ignite his desire to finish *The Man in White*, an historical novel about the Apostle Paul whom Cash identified with deeply.

On Christmas Day 1985, Johnny went to the funeral home where his father's body lay in state following months of suffering. Returning home that evening, John went to change his clothes and saw the fireworks he had purchased months before in the hope that his father might be home for the holidays. Deciding that his father could see them even better now, and much to the delight of the grandkids, John lit them off and then went to bed.

That night Johnny had a dream that he was standing out by the road in front of his parents' house as if waiting for someone. A long, bright silver car came over the hill and pulled up at the curb. John watched as the rear door opened and his father got out. With a young man's stride, his father walked toward him.

"I was waiting for you to come home," Johnny said, reaching out his hand. Suddenly, a long row of light streamed up from the ground between them. His father smiled a knowing smile as the stream of light between them widened and grew brighter. John knew he could not touch him.

"Are you coming inside?" Johnny asked. "Mama would like for you to."

"No, Son," his father replied, still smiling. "I'm afraid it would just cause more pain for everyone. Tell your mother that I just couldn't come back. I'm so comfortable and so happy where I am. I just don't belong here anymore."

"All right," John said and somehow knew it was all right.

Then the light grew so intense Johnny could no longer see his father through it. All of a sudden the light, his father, and the bright silver car were gone, and the only thing in the yard were the spent fireworks from that evening.

"I was never privileged to have an experience like Paul did just outside Damascus," Johnny Cash wrote in *The Man in White*, "but on Christmas night 1985 I had that visionlike dream and saw a light that was unearthly and much more beautiful than the whole box of fireworks."

CHAPTER 19

An Old Man's Final Task

JOHN LOOKED OUT ON THE vast ocean that surrounded Patmos and reflected on a life that felt like it belonged to someone else.

He had been the youngest of the twelve, almost more boy than man. But that was long ago. Now with the death of Thomas, he was the last apostle still alive, the only one still waiting to make that final voyage.

And what of the three years he had spent with the Lord? On days when his solitude and exile seemed a heavy burden, he sometimes wondered if his memories of Jesus were just a trick his aging mind played on him to ease his suffering.

As the sun dipped below the horizon, a cold breeze came off the sea. Feeling the chill, John scrambled back to his hut, lit his small fire, and prepared his simple supper. When it was ready, he knelt and prayed, finishing with the words he said every night: "Even so, Lord, come quickly."

After eating, there was little to do but go to bed. Another day over. As he gazed into the dying embers, John wrestled with the loneliness and the despair that always seemed worse in the hour before sleep as the darkness grew around him. Why does God allow me to go on living? he often thought. What was the point? What purpose was there in another month, another week, another day?

"How long, Lord?" he cried to the empty night. "How long?"

Only silence answered, and slowly his anguish subsided. As he rolled over to try to sleep, he suddenly realized that it was Sunday, the Lord's Day! And he had forgotten to keep it.

Leaping up, John lit the lamp with the precious oil now saved only for special occasions, and began with words the Lord had taught them.

Our Father who art in Heaven, hallowed be thy name. Thy kingdom come. Thy will be done on earth as it is in heaven. Give me this day my daily bread. And forgive me my trespasses as I forgive those who have trespassed against me. And lead me not into temptation, but deliver me from evil. For thine is the kingdom, the power, and the glory....

With this phrase, suddenly the room was filled with the Shekhinah glory of the Lord, brighter than the sun. As John bowed in awe and reverence before the Risen Christ, he heard the words: "I am the Alpha and the Omega, who is, and was, and is to come. Take a pen and write to the seven churches...."

Alone and in exile, John had not been forgotten. The Lord had one more task He wanted him to do.

In 1980, at the age of 48, Johnny Cash became the Country Music Hall of Fame's youngest living inductee. But as the 1980s progressed, more and more it began to seem that his recording career was all but over. Although he still had a decent audience for his live concerts, his record sales were at rock bottom, and Columbia, his record label of nearly 30 years, dropped him.

Then John met Rick Rubin, who up until then had produced music that sounded about as unlike Johnny Cash as music could sound.

"What're you gonna do with me that nobody else has done to sell records for me?" Cash asked.

"Well, I don't know that we *will* sell records," Rubin answered. "I would like you to go with me and sit in my living room with a guitar and two microphones and just sing to your heart's content, everything you ever wanted to record."

"That sounds good to me," Cash replied.

When *American Recordings* was released in the spring of 1994, the praise was unanimous. *Rolling Stone* gave it five stars, and the CD went on to win a Grammy for Best Contemporary Folk Album. And so began Johnny Cash's revival. It was a resurgence that would continue until John's death and beyond, and would produce a series of six highly acclaimed *American Recordings* with Rick Rubin. The partnership also produced what some see as Johnny's most prophetic gospel tracks—songs such as "The Man Comes Around," "God's Gonna Cut You Down," and "Ain't No Grave."

Even more than the music they made together, the two men discovered that they were kindred spirits and developed an intense friendship.

"Working with Johnny was one of the true gifts of my life," Rubin later recalled. "He was so thoughtful and humble, so wise and spiritual. I am so lucky to have had the years we did together."

And so just when it seemed that his career was over, Johnny Cash found that like the Apostle John, he, too, had something more to do and went on to make some of the most compelling music of his life.

CHAPTER 20

The Man Comes Around

"**THE MAN COMES AROUND**" is the title track from *American IV*, which was released in 2002. It was one of the last songs Johnny Cash wrote before his death, and also one of his most prophetic with many sections taken directly from Biblical passages that speak of Christ's Second Coming.

> And I heard, as it were, the noise of thunder
> One of the four beasts saying, "Come and see."
> And I saw, and behold a white horse.
> And I heard a voice in the midst of the four beasts
> And I looked and behold, a pale horse
> And his name that sat on him was Death
> And Hell followed with him.
> *From Revelation, Chapter 6*

Whoever is unjust let him be unjust still.
Whoever is righteous let him be righteous still.
Whoever is filthy let him be filthy still.
From Revelation, Chapter 22

It is hard for thee to kick against the pricks.
From Acts, Chapter 26

THE PARABLE OF THE WISE AND FOOLISH VIRGINS

Then the kingdom of heaven shall be likened to ten virgins who took their lamps and went out to meet the bridegroom. Now five of them were wise, and five were foolish. Those who were foolish took their lamps and took no oil with them, but the wise took oil in their vessels with their lamps. But while the bridegroom was delayed, they all slumbered and slept.

And at midnight a cry was heard: "Behold, the bridegroom is coming. Go out to meet him!" Then all ten virgins arose and trimmed their lamps.

And the foolish said to the wise, "Give us some of your oil, for our lamps are going out." But the wise answered, saying, "No, lest there should not be enough for us and you; but go rather to those who sell, and buy for yourselves." And while they went to buy, the bridegroom came, and those who were ready went in with him to the wedding; and the door was shut.

Afterward the other virgins came also, saying, "Lord, Lord, open to us!" But he answered and said, "I say to you, I do not know you."

> Watch therefore, for you know neither the day nor the hour
> in which the Son of Man is coming.
> ***From Matthew 25:13***

On June 4, 2003, Johnny Cash, weakened by age and illness and now living in the Momma Cash house because of its lack of stairs, honored a request to sing the great Merle Haggard song "Sing Me Back Home."

The words tell the story of a dying man's final request for a song that will turn back the years and make his old memories come alive, a song that, as he puts it, will "sing me back home before I die."

Johnny Cash died at approximately 2:00 in the morning on September 12, 2003. He was buried alongside June in Hendersonville Memory Gardens not far from their beloved lake house in Hendersonville, Tennessee.

"Ain't No Grave" (written by Claude Ely in 1934) was recorded by Johnny Cash several months before his death and was released in 2010 on *American VI*.

AIN'T NO GRAVE

> There ain't no grave can hold my body down.
> There ain't no grave can hold my body down.
> When I hear that trumpet sound I'm gonna rise
> right out of the ground.
> Ain't no grave can hold my body down.

CONCLUSION

An Insider's Look…

JOHNNY'S FINAL DAYS
Based on the Personal Log of Jimmy Tittle

WITH EACH SONG THAT JOHNNY CASH recorded during the last six months of his life, we get more of the sense of a man getting ready to go. The songs he chose for this final chapter of a long career live on as encouragement to those still living and as a caution for us to take stock of what is really important in life.

On April 22, 2003, John recorded "Help Me" at the studio that had been set up in the Mama Cash house where he and June had moved after the stairs in the Lake House across the street became too difficult for them to manage. Originally written by Larry Gatlin,

"Help Me" would become the first track on *American V: A Hundred Highways*, released posthumously in 2006. In the song, John confesses he is tired of walking all alone and asks the Lord to help him walk just one more mile. Here Cash is at his most vulnerable as on bended knees he tells God, "I'm begging you please for help."

The following day he recorded "Another Man Done Gone" and "I Came to Believe." In "I Came to Believe" Johnny tells the personal story of how he could not manage the problem—apparently his pill problem—that he "brought on" himself. Admitting that he needed help, he declares that he has finally surrendered to a power higher than himself. Three years later, this song would also appear on *American V*.

Everyone who knew the couple had always believed it would be Johnny who would go to his reward first, but it was not to be. June Carter Cash passed away on May 15, 2003. Eleven days later in the first session after June's death, Jimmy Tittle would write in the log that he kept, "John did a good job and hurts so much. I don't know how he's doing it. God love him."

Johnny Cash would live without his beloved companion for another four months. During that time—in his illness, in his blindness, and confined to a wheelchair—he turned even more urgently to his music, surrounded by those he loved but missing June, the love of his life.

On May 29, John recorded "I Just Can't Keep From Crying" and "Standing in the Need of Prayer" at the Lake House. In the African-American spiritual sung by so many down through the years, Johnny confesses:

> Not my mother or my father,
> but it's me, O Lord,
> standing in the need of prayer.
> Not my brother or my sister,
> but it's me, O Lord,
> standing in the need of prayer.

Of all the songs Johnny left behind from these final days, perhaps none was more serene than his adaptation of 1 Corinthians 15:55, which he recorded on June 3. He puts to music the passage where St. Paul asks, "O Death, where is thy sting? O Grave, where is thy victory?" And in the final lines tells of how hope springs eternal as just over the hill he sees his redeemer beckoning him.

On June 4, Johnny recorded Merle Haggard's wistful "Sing Me Back Home"—a song that Johnny had sung with Merle years before on *The Johnny Cash Show* on August 2, 1969. The song ends with the request:

> Make my old memories come alive,
> Take me away and turn back the years,
> Sing me back home before I die.

On July 10, John recorded his poignant versions of the traditional American gospel songs "Ain't No Grave" and "I Can't Help But Wonder Where I'm Bound" written by Tom Paxton. Both songs would be included on *American VI* with "Ain't No Grave" serving as the title track.

Four days later John recorded "I'll See You Again," a song written by Jimmy Tittle, Johnny's son-in-law. Jimmy had sung this song for him at the Mama Cash house during his last days, and he would sing it again at the Johnny Cash Memorial Tribute taped just three months later on November 10 at Nashville's Ryman Auditorium.

On July 17, Johnny recorded "His Eye Is on the Sparrow," a song written in 1905 and based on the passage in Matthew 10:29-31 where Jesus tells His followers: "Are not two sparrows sold for a penny? Yet not one of them will fall to the ground outside your Father's care.... So don't be afraid; you are worth more than many sparrows."

In the well-known refrain, the speaker rejoices in the certainty that God cares for him:

> I sing because I'm happy,
> I sing because I'm free,
> For His eye is on the sparrow,
> And I know He watches me.

On August 4, Johnny recorded "I Don't Hurt Anymore," a song originally made famous by Hank Snow. He also recorded "Redemption Day" written by Sheryl Crow.

On August 26, after suffering from stomach pains, Johnny was admitted to Baptist Hospital with pancreatitis. He was released on September 10 feeling well enough to think about making plans later in the month to fly to Los Angeles to do some more recording in Rick Rubin's studio.

"I don't have any fear of death," Cash wrote in the afterword to the paperback edition of his autobiography that was released after he was diagnosed with Shy-Drager syndrome. "I'm very much at peace with myself and with my God. I accept this disease because it's the will of God; it's Him working in my life. And when He sees fit to take me from this world, I'll be reunited with some good people I haven't seen for a while."

On September 11, Johnny recorded "I'll See You Again" and "I'm Sorry, Lord." That afternoon he was taken by ambulance back to the hospital, this time with serious respiratory problems. That night, John Carter, Rosanne, and Kathy kept vigil. At approximately 2 in the morning on September 12, 2003, Johnny Cash crashed through Heaven's door.

And then the circle truly was unbroken.

OXVISION
BOOKS